a girl's guide to
Heavenly Mother

Written by McArthur Krishna & Bethany Brady Spalding

Art by: Allen TenBusschen, Ashmae Hoiland, Ben Crowder, Caitlin Connolly, Claire Tollstrup, Courtney Vander Veur Matz, Esther Candari Christiansen, Heather Ruttan, J. Kirk Richards, Jenedy Paige, Joumana Borderie, Kathy Peterson, Katrina Berg, Kwani Povi Winder, Laura Erekson, Lisa DeLong, Louise Parker, McArthur Krishna, Melissa Kamba Boggs, Michelle Franzoni Thorley, Michelle Gessell, Normandie Shael Luscher, Paige Anderson, Rachel Hunt Steenblick, Richard Lasisi Olagunju, Sherron Valeña Crisanto, Sopheap Nhem, Susana Silva

Glorious thanks to the many LDS artists from around the world who have generously shared their vision of Heavenly Mother.

d D Street
PRESS

What you'll find inside
A Girl's Guide to Heavenly Mother...

This guide is filled with truths, tips, quotes, questions, and amazing art to help you: →

Artist: Kathy Peterson

KNOW YOUR HEAVENLY MOTHER

#1 Goddess

#2 Equal in might and glory

#3 All-powerful

#4 Soul Shaper

#5 Creator

#6 Caring Companion

#7 Loving Parent

UNDERSTAND MAGNIFICENT TRUTHS ABOUT YOURSELF

#1 You are made in Her image

#2 You have a matriarchal lineage

#3 You have an ultimate female role model

#4 You are a goddess in the making

CREATE CHANGE FOR A MORE LOVING WORLD

#1 In yourself

#2 In your family

#3 In your church community

#4 Throughout the whole world

Artist: Kathy Peterson

Let's illuminate our lives by sharing the doctrine of Heavenly Mother!

66 I have heard it said by some that the reason women in the Church struggle to know themselves is because they don't have a divine female role model. But we do. We believe we have a mother in heaven... Furthermore, I believe we know much more about our eternal nature than we think we do; and it is our **sacred obligation** to express our knowledge, to teach it to our young sisters and daughters... 99

– Patricia Holland, former counselor in the Young Women general presidency

Artist: Caitlin Connolly

To all the girls in the world—

Tiny ones, toddlers, little kids, big kids, tweens, teens, young adults, thirty somethings, middle-agers, grandmas, grande dames, and beyond...

As you journey through womanhood, here are three very important truths to guide you:

1 You are divine.

2 You are a daughter of Heavenly Mother and Heavenly Father, who love you always.

3 You are a goddess in the making!

<u>Being a woman is phenomenal</u>—you have extraordinary power, passion, and potential. However, there might be days that don't feel all that grand. Understanding who you *truly* are will help you navigate the twists and turns and twirly loops along the path of womanhood.

This guidebook is designed to help you know your Heavenly Mother, understand magnificent truths about yourself, and create change for a more loving world. So turn the page and let's begin...

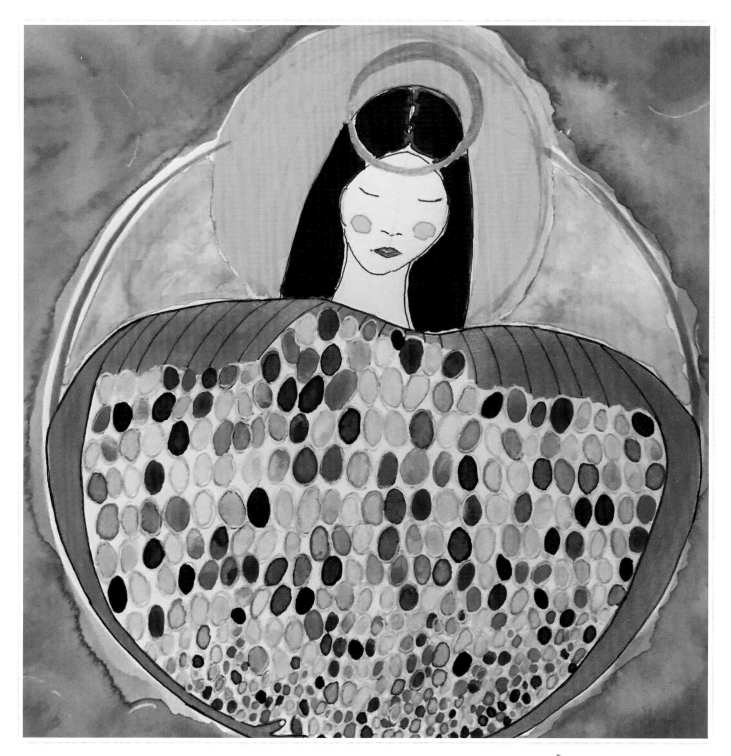

Artist: Michelle Gessell

DIVINE ATTRIBUTE #1

Goddess

Here's a thrilling truth: Heavenly Mother is a God—just like Heavenly Father!

Through modern-day revelation, we know that God is actually Heavenly Father AND Heavenly Mother **UNITED**.

> "Deity consists of man and woman...there can be no God except he is composed of the man and woman united, and there is not in all the eternities that exist, or ever will be a God in any other way."
> – Elder Erastus Snow

WOW. Isn't that amazing? And why is knowing that amazing doctrine so important?

A common belief in the world is that God is male. But we know that God is actually both Heavenly Mother and Heavenly Father. And this changes our world! Knowing about Heavenly Mother enlightens and expands our view of Deity. This doctrine allows us, as girls and women, to see ourselves in God. **And that's important**.

According to the Prophet Joseph Smith, in order to understand ourselves, we need to clearly know the true and full nature of God.

SO LET'S ALWAYS REMEMBER—"GOD" MEANS HEAVENLY PARENTS!

NEED TO KNOW:

The Old Testament was written in Hebrew. In that language, one of the words for God—"Elohim"—is actually a plural word.

ELOHIM=GODS! ⟵

So the word God in the Old Testament could sometimes refer to both Heavenly Parents. The word Elohim appears over 2,500 times in the Old Testament... it's exciting to see how Heavenly Mother might be found throughout the scriptures!

Artist: Richard Lasisi Olagunju

Artist: Heather Ruttan

HOW DO THESE TRUTHS CHANGE THE WAY YOU THINK ABOUT GOD AND YOURSELF?

Equal in Might & Glory

DIVINE ATTRIBUTE #2

As a Goddess, Heavenly Mother is equal in might and glory to Heavenly Father!

"The divine Mother, side by side with the divine Father, [has] the equal sharing of equal rights, privileges and responsibilities."
– Sister Susa Young Gates*

So what does that bold statement actually mean? Let's break it down:

1 Heavenly Mother has the same godly traits as Heavenly Father...She is like Him "in glory, perfection, compassion, wisdom, and holiness."**

2 Heavenly Mother works side by side with Heavenly Father to love and bless Their children.

3 Our Heavenly Parents are a perfect example of equal partnership.***

EQUALITY IS DIVINE.
How awesome is that?

> **No matter to what heights God has attained or may attain, he does not stand alone; for side by side with him, in all her glory, a glory like unto his, stands a companion, the Mother of his children. For as we have a Father in heaven, so also we have a Mother there, a glorified, exalted, ennobled Mother.**
>
> – Elder Melvin J. Ballard

*Susa was the daughter of the Prophet Brigham Young and the founder of two publications that became the official magazines for the Young Women and Relief Society organizations.

**Encyclopedia of Mormonism   ***The Family: A Proclamation to the World

All-powerful

HOW DOES KNOWING THAT YOUR HEAVENLY MOTHER IS A STRONG AND ALL-POWERFUL WOMAN HELP YOU TACKLE YOUR OWN HARD CHALLENGES?

Want to learn a new word? **OMNIPOTENT!** Omnipotent means all-powerful. And, as Elder Uchtdorf taught, "We are the literal spirit children of divine, immortal, and **omnipotent** Heavenly Parents!"

So that means Heavenly Mother and Heavenly Father can do **ANYTHING**.

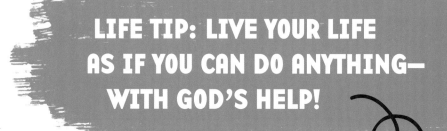

LIFE TIP: LIVE YOUR LIFE AS IF YOU CAN DO ANYTHING— WITH GOD'S HELP!

 With God all things are possible.
– Matthew 19:26

Artist: Allen
TenBusschen

> 66 **We are part of a divine plan designed by Heavenly Parents who love us.** 99
>
> – President M. Russell Ballard

Artist: Ben Crowder

Soul Shaper

Here's a truth that will make you shout for joy:

Just like Heavenly Father, Heavenly Mother has always been with you! As the mother of your spirit, She nurtured you in heaven until you were ready to come to earth. Heavenly Mother is a soul shaper.

NEED TO KNOW:

Heavenly Mother co-designed the Plan of Salvation with Heavenly Father. She wanted to give you (and all of Her children) the chance to ride camels, dance the flamenco, score soccer goals, build friendships, and create families. Our Heavenly Parents wanted you to practice conquering challenges, loving deeply, learning fascinating things, and so much more.

HOW DOES IT MAKE YOU FEEL TO KNOW YOU HAVE A HEAVENLY MOTHER WHO ADORES YOU AND DELIGHTS IN YOUR GROWTH?

You should know about an LDS scholar named Martin Pulido. He writes about Heavenly Mother so beautifully.

> " There is a woman who **shaped my soul**, who cares and loves me, and who is helping govern this world. She watches the sparrow; She watches each grain of sand and star in the sky; She watches the lilies; She watches me. She is by my side, and She is helping me become all that I can be. "
>
> – Martin Pulido

15

> **66** In the ongoing process of creation—our creation and the creation of all that surrounds us—our heavenly parents are preparing a lovely tapestry with exquisite colors and patterns and hues. They are doing so lovingly and carefully and masterfully. **99**
>
> – Patricia Holland, former counselor in the general Young Women presidency

Artist: J. Kirk Richards

Creator

DIVINE ATTRIBUTE #5

Our Heavenly Parents wanted us to have an earthly home *"to please the eye and to gladden the heart...and to enliven the soul."* Isn't it fun to think of Heavenly Mother's role in creating the earth? Maybe Her hands crafted...

D&C 59:18-19

- ○ the kangaroos and the craggy coastal cliffs of Australia
- ○ the hot tangerine sand dunes of the Sahara
- ○ the rushing rivers of West Virginia
- ○ the cobalt blue of a peacock's head
- ○ the snow-capped peaks of the Himalayas
- ○ the pokey spindles of a protea flower
- ○ the enchanting Jacaranda tree of Latin America
- ○ _____
- ○ _____
- ○ _____

Add some of your favorite creations here

LIFE TIP:

Honor Heavenly Mother by taking care of creation. Be thoughtful of how your life choices impact the earth: waste less, bike more, eat meat sparingly. (Follow the Word of Wisdom!) Take actions that matter to you.

A Caring Companion

Do you know that Heavenly Mother is **involved in your daily life** NOW? It's true! She is a wonderful companion through your earthly experience. Heavenly Mother is constantly trying to help you—she can inspire you, guide you, and protect you.

Heavenly Mother and Heavenly Father even sent Their Son, Jesus, to set an example for you. That's how much They care!

Every day our Heavenly Mother is concerned about what you're doing and can reach out to intervene in your life. The Prophet Harold B. Lee once told a story about how Heavenly Mother stopped a man from smoking. And just like She cared for that man's well-being, She cares for *yours*. Heavenly Mother cares about everything you do!

LIFE TIP:

Ponder Heavenly Mother's influence in your life. When you think about the hand of God in your life, remember Heavenly Mother's loving hands.

> 66 ...we have a Heavenly Father and a Heavenly Mother who are even more concerned, probably, than our earthly father and mother...influences from beyond are constantly working to try to help us. 99
>
> – Prophet Harold B. Lee

Artist: Esther Candari Christiansen

"Our Heavenly Parents' love and concern for us continues to this very moment."

– President M. Russell Ballard

"There is an exalted woman, the Mother of your spirit, who cares, instructs, and watches over you, who is helping govern the universe. There is someone on your side, urging you to become all you can be, who sent Her son along with the Father to help show you the way... That's powerful."

– Martin Pulido, LDS scholar

> **❝On a particularly difficult day, or sometimes a series of difficult days, what would this world's inhabitants pay to know that heavenly parents are reaching across...streams and mountains and deserts, anxious to hold them close?❞**
>
> – Elder Jeffrey R. Holland

Artist: Courtney Vander Veur Matz

 **DIVINE ATTRIBUTE #7**

Loving Parent

Heavenly Mother has a heart as wide as eternity!

She cares when you feel lonely.
She cares when you fall short.
She cares when you hurt.

Heavenly Mother is with you on your down days. And on the days that you shine with success, She's celebrating right alongside you.

She leaps for joy when you are **kind**.
She leaps for joy when you are **brave**.
She leaps for joy when you **reach for your eternal potential**.

And even on the in-between days, Heavenly Mother is feeling for you. She is your perfectly loving Mom!

HOW DOES IT FEEL TO KNOW YOUR HEAVENLY MOTHER IS ALWAYS BY YOUR SIDE?

 > **Do you think our Heavenly Parents want us to succeed? Yes! They want us to succeed gloriously. And do you think They will help us? Absolutely!**
>
> – President Jean B. Bingham, former general Relief Society president

> **Heavenly Mother isn't taking a break while Her kids are away at school. Heavenly Mother spends Her days and nights serving us. She mourns with us. She comforts us. She encourages us. She strengthens us. She actively plays a crucial role in the plan of salvation. She matters, and because She matters, I, and all of Her daughters, matter.**
>
> – Rosemary Card, CEO and author

You are like Her

This far into the guidebook, you now know a lot about Heavenly Mother. But how does all of that knowledge relate to YOU?

Elder Holland offers a key...you may want to stop and read his words a few times to let them sink in.

> **❝** I want you to...**know who you truly are.** You are literally a spirit daughter of heavenly parents with a divine nature and an eternal destiny. That surpassing truth should be **fixed deep in your soul and be fundamental to every decision you make as you grow into mature womanhood. ❞**

 SO LET'S EXPLORE SOME MAGNIFICENT TRUTHS ABOUT YOU...

Artist: Lisa DeLong

22

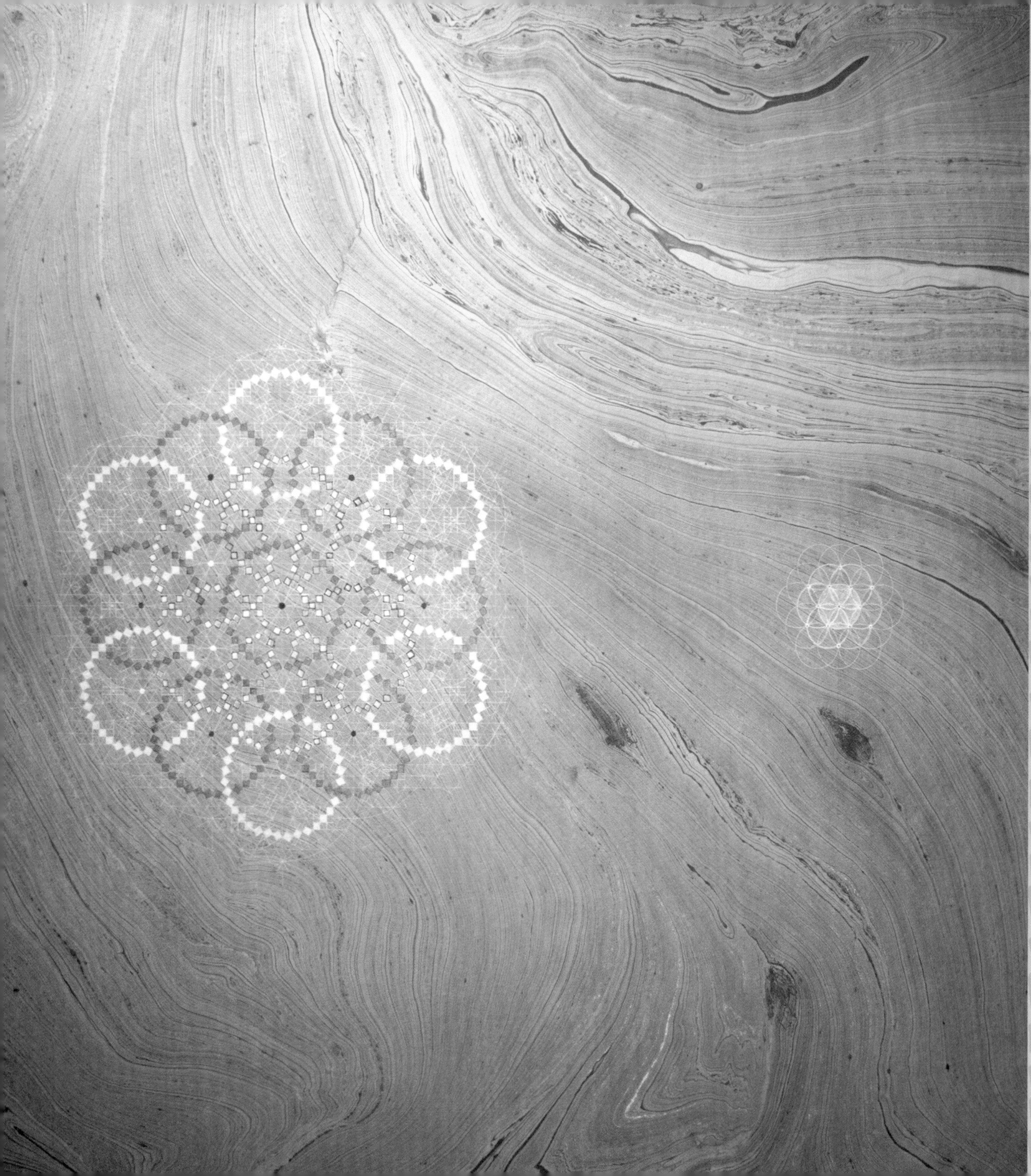

You are made in Her image

You are created in your Heavenly Mother's image—both your body and spirit.

Your body is exquisite! No matter your shape, size, or skin color, you are created in the image of Heavenly Mother. Your curves and creative forces are spectacular and sacred. Your body has a divine design. Your brain, your breasts, your hips, your womb—in all their varieties—are powerful womanly parts.

You may not feel that way every day...and that's ok. But try to **embrace your body as a gift from your Heavenly Parents**, rather than criticize and complain about it.

And remember: who you are is way more than just a body! Your spirit is also made in Heavenly Mother's image. Close your eyes. Take a deep breath. Ponder how your spirit is like your Heavenly Mother's.

> **"You are daughters of God... You are made in the image of our heavenly mother."**
>
> – Prophet Spencer W. Kimball

NEED TO KNOW:

The images you see of women in magazines and other media are often extremely edited to look perfect. These images are not real, but they can impact how you think and feel about your own body. Choose to be confident! Refuse to dislike your body. Refuse to compare it to others'. Claim your body as the exquisite gift that it is.

Artist: Melissa Kamba Boggs

WHAT DO YOU LOVE ABOUT YOUR UNIQUE BODY & SPIRIT?

You have a matriarchal lineage

You come from a matriarchal line—full of women who have great gifts and goodness. They are colorful, complex, imperfect women with fascinating stories of choices and challenges and triumphs. You have mothers and grandmothers, and they have mothers and grandmothers, all the way back to Mother Eve.

You've inherited divine traits from your Heavenly Mother, as well as from all the women who came before you. You come from a long lineage of love.

66 **Have you ever been told you are just like your mother, or you have your father's smile, or all of your family have the same color of eyes? The physical characteristics that we inherit from our parents are obvious. The spiritual characteristics we inherit from our heavenly parents have to be developed.** 99

– Elaine L. Jack, former Relief Society general president

LIFE TIP: Talk to your family, learn about your ancestors, and write down your own matriarchal line... your name, your mother's name, your grandmothers', your great grandmothers'.

_____

_____

_____

_____

_____

❝ **We are children of God with a spirit lineage to Heavenly Parents.** ❞

— President Dallin H. Oaks

❝ **I possess in embryo all that made Mother Eve, as well as our heavenly Mother, good, gracious, and divine.** ❞

— Susa Young Gates

Artist: Michelle Franzoni Thorley

27

You have an ultimate female role model

No matter what your family history hands you, YOU get to decide who you want to be in this life! There are so many remarkable women in the world to look up to...your moms, stepmoms, aunts, grandmas, teachers, neighbors, church leaders, artists, activists, athletes, musicians, writers, inventors, entrepreneurs, politicians, business women, and more. These women are **inspiring**.

In addition to all of these women, remember to also look up to your Heavenly Mother. She can be your ultimate female role model. **She is all that you can become!**

YOUR MAGNIFICENT TRUTH #3

LIFE TIP:
Turn your role models into mentors by building friendships, asking them lots of questions, taking notes, and learning from them along your life's journey. Good women can teach us many important traits of Heavenly Mother.

REMEMBER PATRICIA HOLLAND'S WISE WORDS AT THE BEGINNING OF THE GUIDEBOOK (PAGE 4/5).

66 **Our highest aspiration is to become like our heavenly parents.** 99

President Dallin H. Oaks

Artist: Normandie Shael Luscher

❝You are a perfect version of Heavenly Mother. Your destiny is not counselor-hood. Your destiny is Godhood.❞

– Michael A. Goodman,
Professor of Religion
at Brigham Young
University

Artist: Louise Parker

You Are a Goddess ⟫⟫⟫ In the Making

YOUR MAGNIFICENT TRUTH #4

The Prophet Lorenzo Snow taught an astounding truth: ★ **"As man now is, God once was; as God now is, man may be."** ★ So what does this astounding truth mean for you as a young woman?

All of your life experiences are preparing you to be a GODDESS. That's **HUGE. STUNNING. INCREDIBLE.**

And, you are already on your way...
enjoy this poem by Rachel Hunt Steenblick:

> ❝ [A]s begotten children of heavenly parents, we are endowed with the potential to become like them, just as mortal children may become like their mortal parents. ❞
>
> – Prophet Russell M. Nelson

"LIKE HER"

Many of us already
give life like Her,
give birth to artwork,
children, and ideas.
Many of us are already
brave like Her
doing things that take
our whole heart and
our whole courage.
Many of us are already
strong like Her
lifting the things that
need to be lifted,
carrying them until
it's time to set
them down.
Many of us already
love like Her–
the world with its beauty,
giving, and imperfections,
people with theirs, too.

HOW ARE YOU ALREADY LIKE HER?

You Are a Goddess!

IN THE MAKING

Artist: Laura Erekson

Turning truth into action

> 66 It is not enough that theology help me to understand God. It must also help me to understand myself and my world. 99
>
> – Francine R. Bennion, former member of the Young Women and Relief Society general boards

So what do you *do* with all of these truths you've discovered in this guidebook? You now know **7 Divine Attributes of Heavenly Mother** and **4 Magnificent Truths about Yourself**.

And truth is **POWERFUL**! Truth can change you, your family, and even the world around you.

WHAT STEPS CAN YOU TAKE TO PUT THESE TRUTHS INTO ACTION? (PSSST: KEEP READING—THERE ARE TIPS AHEAD!)

Artist: Susana Silva

In yourself

You can invite Heavenly Mother into your spiritual life!

TOP 10 IDEAS

1. Try to recognize Her influence in your life

2. Be grateful for all that She has done for you

3. Be mindful of Her as you read the scriptures

4. Hang artwork in your room that reminds you of Her

5. Think of Her during church services

6. Incorporate Her into hymns and other church songs

7. Search for Her in the temple

8. Mention Her in your prayers

9. Notice Her majestic creations in the world around you

10. Read more about Her (You can begin with the reference section at the back of this guidebook. Then continue your search at www.SeekingHeavenlyMother.com.)

Write your own ideas here:

_____

_____

_____

_____

_____

_____

_____

_____

_____

_____

_____

_____

_____

_____

_____

_____

_____

Artist: Paige Anderson

In Your Family

You can use the truths about Heavenly Mother to strengthen your family in many different ways. Here are a few ideas to get you started:

1 Share your own thoughts on Heavenly Mother with your family.

2 Discuss the truths from this book in a Family Home Evening, around the dinner table, or on a long car ride. (Learning about Heavenly Mother is important for your dad and brothers too!)

3 Reflect on Divine Attribute #2 (on pages 10-11) and ask yourself:

> Are you practicing divine equality in your family?

> In what ways could you and your siblings more equally share the responsibilities and the fun of family life?

> What skills can you develop *now* to help you create an equal partnership in the future?

> How can you tell that the boys you date would value their wife as an equal partner?

> Your thoughts here...

LIFE TIP: BE GOOD TO YOUR MOM.

66 **Within every human body dwells a living spirit born to our loving, eternal heavenly parents. When parents know this, they can better guide their families by focusing upon the eternal relationships and the true purposes of this life.** 99

– President M. Russell Ballard

Do you know what a "mother tongue" is? That is the language you were born into and that feels the most natural to you. Remember Pulido? (flip back to page 15) He encourages us to develop a "mother tongue" about Heavenly Mother—a sense of comfort, fluency, and ease when we speak of Her.

Artist: Sherron Valeña Crisanto

In Your Church Community

The Young Women theme begins with this truth, **"I am a beloved daughter of Heavenly Parents."** Even with this recited every Sunday around the world, some people are still uncomfortable speaking about Heavenly Mother. But, prophets, apostles, and church leaders do— **so let's follow their lead!** Truths about Heavenly Mother can uplift ourselves and our church community.

So go for it!

In Young Women lessons, in Sunday School discussions, in Relief Society gatherings, in ministering to sisters, in sacrament meeting talks—in every gospel setting that is appropriate—talk about Heavenly Mother. Don't leave Her out!

Come back and jot down your experiences speaking about Heavenly Mother at church:

_____
_____
_____
_____
_____
_____

> **66** The doctrine of a Heavenly Mother is a cherished and distinctive belief among Latter-day Saints. **99**
>
> – Gospel Topics, ChurchofJesusChrist.org

 **CREATE CHANGE #4**

Throughout the whole world

Prophets teach what the world needs to hear.

An apostle Neil A. Maxwell taught, "In this dispensation the Lord gave us this doctrinal truth [of Heavenly Mother] through a Prophet...the basic truths are always the same, but the emphasis needed will be made by living prophets under inspiration from the living God, and the people of the living Church will respond."

Why is the truth of Heavenly Mother **so needed** in our time? Just take a look around...

In some places in the world, women and girls are severely mistreated. They are abused, discriminated against, and viewed as second-class people.

But even in everyday situations across the globe, women are often devalued. Too many women have their opportunities limited, opinions dismissed, bodies desecrated, and their potential overlooked.

It hurts. But this can change by living according to revealed truths!

 What would the world look like if we all honored our Heavenly Mother... and treated girls and women as Her divine daughters?

1 Women would be free from abuse and mistreatment.

2 Women could use their agency to choose their dreams and reach their full potential.

3 Women and men could work together to solve the world's challenges.

Artist: Joumana Borderie

IN WHAT OTHER WAYS WOULD THE WORLD BE BETTER IF WE HONORED OUR HEAVENLY MOTHER AND ALL OF HER DAUGHTERS? WHAT CAN YOU DO TO HELP?

Welcome Home!

*You should read more delightful wisdoms of Chieko Okazaki, former first counselor in the Relief Society general presidency.

After living, learning, and contributing here on earth, you will someday return home to heaven. **There, our Heavenly Mother and Heavenly Father will joyously welcome you with an exuberant embrace!***

Can you imagine being wrapped in the arms of a beaming Heavenly Mother? She'll be elated to see you! And after a life of refining experiences, just think…you will be like Her! But until that time comes, remember to…

Stay close to your Heavenly Mother. She is loving and guiding you on your journey.

66 Sisters, I testify that when you stand in front of your heavenly parents in those royal courts on high and you look into Her eyes and behold Her countenance, any question you ever had about the role of women in the kingdom will evaporate into the rich celestial air, because at that moment you will see standing directly in front of you, your divine nature and destiny. 99

– Elder Glenn L. Pace

44

Artist: Kwani Povi Winder

What does Heavenly Mother mean to you?

Journal here:

_____

_____

_____

_____

_____

_____

_____

_____

_____

_____

_____

_____

_____

Artist: Jenedy Paige

66 Queenly elegance of our Heavenly Mother 99

– Prophet Spencer W. Kimball

Artist: Ashmae Hoiland

Bethany

Bethany calls the colorful river city of Richmond, Virginia home, but she wrote this book on an 8 month family adventure around the world—searching for truth, beauty, and joy on 5 continents and 20 countries. Climbing Himalayan peaks in Bhutan with Andy; jumping and making waves in Australia with Simone; devouring delicacies in Greece with Phoebe; chasing sunsets around Kenya and scootering through France with Brontë; and empowering girls through soccer in India with the whole Brady Spalding team. Who knows what she'll do next?

McArthur

When McArthur was twelve years old, she realized that she believed in Heavenly Mother. That truth has been a guiding light in making decisions about how to spend her life from junior high through graduate school, owning her own business, getting married and having children. This knowledge has steered her to places that value her worth and honor her soul. With a desire for that same light to guide all girls and women, she set out to make this book happen...and here we are. Hallelujah.

Artist and Title of Work

Artist: Katrina Berg

49

References

Page 4-5: Patricia T. Holland, "One Thing Needful," *Ensign*, Oct. 1987, 32.

Page 8-9: Erastus Snow, Journal of Discourses, 19:269–70, March 3, 1878.

Val Larson, "Hidden in Plain View: Mother in Heaven in Scripture," *SquareTwo*, Vol. 8, No. 2 (Summer 2015).

Lectures on Faith [1985], 4.

Page 10-11: Susa Young Gates, "The Vision Beautiful," *Improvement Era* 540, April 1920, 542.

Bryant S. Hinckley, *Sermons and Mission Services of Melvin Joseph Ballard* [1949], 205.

Elaine Anderson Cannon, "Mother in Heaven," *Encyclopedia of Mormonism*, 961.

"The Family: A Proclamation to the World," *Ensign*, Nov. 2010, 129.

Page 12-13: Dieter F. Uchtdorf, "O How Great the Plan of Our God," *Ensign*, Nov. 2016, 21.

Page 14-15: M. Russell Ballard, *When Thou Art Converted: Continuing Our Search for Happiness* [2001], 62.

Danielle B. Wagner, "14 Myths and Truths We Know About Our Heavenly Mother," LDS Living, http://www.ldsliving.com/14-Myths-and-Truths-We-Know-About-Our-Heavenly-Mother/s/88439.

Page 16-17: Patricia T. Holland, "Your Purpose: Filling the Measure of Your Creation" [Brigham Young University Devotional, Jan. 17, 1989], speeches.byu.edu.

Page 18-19: Harold B. Lee, "The Influence and Responsibility of Women," *Relief Society Magazine* 51, no. 2 (Feb. 1964): 85.

M. Russell Ballard, *Our Search for Happiness* [1993], 70.

Danielle B. Wagner, "14 Myths and Truths We Know About Our Heavenly Mother," LDS Living, http://www.ldsliving.com/14-Myths-and-Truths-We-Know-About-Our-Heavenly-Mother/s/88439.

Page 20-21: Jean B. Bingham, "How Vast Is Our Purpose" [Brigham Young University Women's Conference, May 5, 2017], womensconference.byu.edu.

Jeffrey R. Holland, "The Meaning of Membership: A Personal Response," *However Long and Hard the Road*, 1985, p. 40-51.

Rosemary Card, *Model Mormon: Fighting for Self-Worth on the Runway and as an Independent Woman* [2018], 127.

Page 22-23: Jeffrey R. Holland, "To Young Women," *Ensign* or *Liahona*, Nov. 2005, p. 28-30.

Page 24-25: *The Teachings of Spencer W. Kimball*, ed. Edward L. Kimball [1982], p. 25.

Page 26-27: Dallin H. Oaks, "Powerful Ideas," *Ensign*, Nov. 1995, p 25-27.

Elaine L. Jack, "Identity of a Young Woman," *Ensign*, Nov. 1989, p 86-88.

Susa Young Gates, "What my Faith Means to Me," *Juvenile Instructor*, Vol. 53, Issue 6, June 1918, page 291.

Page 28-29: Dallin H. Oaks, "Fundamental to Our Faith," *Ensign* or *Liahona*, Jan. 2011, 23. This article is excerpted from an address given to the faculty and students of Harvard Law School on Feb. 26, 2010.

Page 30-31: Eliza R. Snow, *Biography and Family Record of Lorenzo Snow* [1884], 46-47.

Erica Ostergar, "15 Inspiring Quotes from Education Week 2018," BYU News, https://news.byu.edu/news/15-inspiring-quotes-education-week-2018.

Russell M. Nelson, "Perfection Pending," *Ensign*, Nov. 1995, p. 65-67.

Page 34-35: Francine R. Bennion, "A Latter-day Saint Theology of Suffering," *At the Pulpit: 185 Years of Discourses by Latter-day Saint Women*, Jennifer Reeder & Kate Holbrook (eds.), 217.

Page 38-39: M. Russell Ballard, "Spiritual Development," *Ensign*, Nov. 1978, p. 65-67.

Page 40-41: "Mother in Heaven," Gospel Topics, churchofjesuschrist.org.

Danielle B. Wagner, "14 Myths and Truths We Know About Our Heavenly Mother," LDS Living, http://www.ldsliving.com/14-Myths-and-Truths-We-Know-About-Our-Heavenly-Mother/s/88439.

Page 42-43: Neal A. Maxwell, *Things As They Really Are* [1978], p. 67.

Page 44-45: Glenn L. Pace, "The Divine Nature and Destiny of Women" [Brigham Young University devotional, March 6, 2010], speeches.byu.edu.

Chieko N. Okazaki, *Sanctuary* [1997], 129-130.

Page 47: Spencer W. Kimball "The True Way of Life and Salvation," *Ensign*, May 1978, 4.

Extensive resources can be found here:

◖ David Paulsen and Martin Pulido's article "'A Mother There': A Survey of Historical Teachings about Mother in Heaven," published by BYU Studies www.byustudies.byu.edu/content/mother-there-survey-historical-teachings-about-mother-heaven

◔ www.SeekingHeavenlyMother.com

Artist: Claire Tollstrup

Dedications

For the exquisite delight of being a woman and a creator.
– McArthur

To my own magnificent daughters—Simone, Phoebe, and Brontë; to my gorgeous Greek South African goddaughter—Jessica Hull; and to all daughters around the world...may we all know our strength, power, and divinity. Shine on!
-Bethany

In gratitude for the magnanimous (and funny) Amy who believed, and made this whole thing happen.

Artist: McArthur Krishna

d D Street PRESS

Text copyrighted by D Street Press. All illustration rights are owned by individual artists. First published in USA by D Street Press in 2020. Printed in India. For information about permission to reproduce selections from the book, write howdy@dstreetpress.com.

D Street Press, Portland, OR, 97239 USA.

Edited by Johanna Buchert Smith, Cathy Carmode Lim, Emily Plicka, and Ashley Stahle.

Graphic design and layout by Kate Purcell, katepurcelldesign.com.

ISBN 978-1-7342287-0-0